NATIONAL GEOGRAPHIC

# Ladders

# GREAT PLAINS

## WHERE ON EARTH?

GENRE Social Studies Article

**Read to find out** about the land we call the Great Plains.

# SEA OF Grass

by Sherri Patoka

This is Scotts Bluff in Nebraska. It is part of the Great Plains. Scotts Bluff was one of the major landmarks that early pioneers saw as they journeyed to the West.

The Great Plains is a large, mostly flat region of grasslands that lies between the Midwest and the Rocky Mountains. As you stand in the middle of these plains, you notice that the ground is mostly covered with long grasses. This is called a **prairie**. There are almost no trees to block the distant view, so the sky seems huge.

When the wind blows across the prairie, the long grasses roll like waves. It looks like you're in the middle of a sea of grass. There are places on the prairie where the grasses are taller than a person.

But not every part of the Great Plains is flat and grassy. As pioneers traveled westward over the plains, they looked ahead for Scotts Bluff (pictured here). Scotts Bluff is a group of buttes. A **butte** (BYOOT) is a steep hill with a flat top. It looks like a mountain with its top cut off. After traveling for weeks on the flat prairies, pioneers were glad to see buttes rising from the plains.

# Where on Earth?

## THE GREAT PLAINS

As you can tell from this map, the Great Plains region covers parts of ten states in the middle of the United States. There is a lot to explore in this land of long grasses gently rolling under a big sky.

### Wyoming

Devils Tower in Wyoming was the first national monument in the United States. It rises more than 1,200 feet above the prairie. It's a mass of hard volcanic rock that rose up through the ground millions of years ago. The rock around it wore away, leaving its cracked side and flat top.

### Kansas

Prairie dogs have their own towns! They live underground throughout the Great Plains. These little animals are expert tunnel diggers. They build each room for a reason. They have sleeping rooms and toilet rooms. Prairie dogs even have rooms to listen for danger outside. You can visit them at Prairie Dog State Park in Kansas.

## The Oregon Trail

In the 1840s, most people in the United States lived in the East. People began moving west, looking for land and adventure. The Oregon Trail stretched from the Missouri River to western Oregon. Thousands of people traveled this trail in groups of covered wagons called wagon trains.

## Nebraska

Can you imagine giant pigs and small rhinos roaming the middle of the United States? Millions of years ago, different kinds of animals roamed the prairies. There were even beardogs. These fierce animals were almost as big as wolves! Fossils from the Ashfall Fossil Beds in Nebraska paint a picture of what life was like long, long ago. These workers are uncovering the bones of a rhinoceros that lived 10 million years ago.

## Oklahoma

Some pioneers wanted to settle on the Great Plains. But without trees for wood, they needed different kinds of materials to build homes. The answer was sod, the thick prairie surface soil held together by grass roots. Only a few sod houses remain today. You can see them at the Sod House Museum in Oklahoma.

**Check In** What words can you use to describe the Great Plains?

**GENRE** Economics Article **Read to find out** about farming on the Great Plains.

# From Field to

*by Cynthia Clampitt*

Farming is important on the Great Plains. You can see why when you look at these Kansas wheat fields. The gold areas in this photo are all wheat fields ready for harvest.

# Table

If you were flying in a plane across the Great Plains, what would you see? The land below you would look like a checkerboard. Each square is a farm growing a different crop. There might be a few brown patches on the checkerboard where the farmers haven't planted yet. That is **topsoil**, the rich top layer of soil in which plants grow. The topsoil of the Great Plains is some of the deepest and richest in the world. Plenty of sunshine and an underground water supply make this land perfect for farming.

The Great Plains region has been called the breadbasket of the United States. That's because so much of the nation's wheat crop is grown here. Wheat is ground into flour, which is then used to make bread and many other foods. But wheat isn't the only food grown here. Corn, soybeans, sugar beets, and many other crops grow well on the Great Plains.

In spring, farmers plow the fields and plant the crops. Summer sun and rain help the crops grow. Late summer and autumn is the time for harvesting, or picking the crops. Farmers of the Great Plains help to feed people all over the world!

# Bring on the Machines

In the early 1800s, an explorer named Zebulon Pike went to check out the country's western lands. He claimed that the western prairies were impossible to farm. The sod, or the grasses and their roots, formed a tough layer that couldn't be broken up for planting. There wasn't enough water, either. Too bad he couldn't see the huge source of underground water, which would make growing crops easier. And too bad he hadn't met John Deere.

In 1837, a blacksmith named John Deere invented a steel plow that could "bust" through the sod. The farmers who used it became known as **sodbusters**.

Things have changed a lot for farmers since the days of John Deere. The hard work of farming has become easier with bigger and better equipment. Farming the land still takes a lot of time and work. But today's monster machines make the job easier—and a little more fun.

Farmers work on huge tractors that have tires taller than a grown man. These tractors weigh as much as 10 cars!

Huge machines such as this combine (KOM-byn) make the farmer's job easier. A combine cuts the wheat, separates the grain from the rest of the plant, and cleans it. One machine does it all.

# The Big Three

The Great Plains farmers grow lots of different crops. But the "big three" are corn, wheat, and soybeans. In one growing season, they go from tiny seeds to plants in the field to food on your table.

## CORN

More American farmers grow corn than any other crop. The Great Plains state of Iowa grows more corn than any other state. A typical Iowa corn plant can grow to be eight feet tall.

You may have eaten corn on the cob before. Did you know that corn can be boiled down to make a sweet syrup?

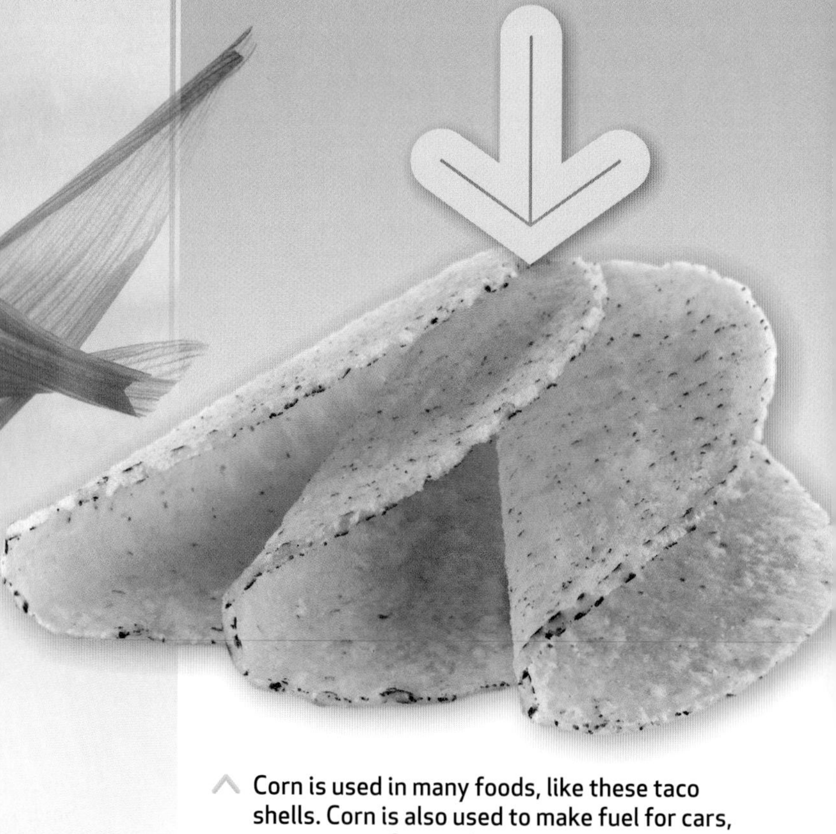

Corn is used in many foods, like these taco shells. Corn is also used to make fuel for cars, a sweetener for toothpaste, and ingredients in paint, vitamins, and even spark plugs!

# WHEAT

Individual grains that grow on stems of wheat are called kernels. There are about 50 kernels on one stem.

The wheat your pizza dough is made with was originally brought to the Americas by European settlers. It was an easy crop to grow.

Wheat is ground into flour and used to make cereals and baked goods such as bread. We eat only the grains. The stalks are used in straw for animal bedding—and in making paper.

# SOYBEANS

Have you ever eaten *edamame* (eh-duh-MAH-may)? *Edamame* is the Japanese word for soybean.

Farmers change where they plant their crops every few years. Replacing corn or wheat fields with soybeans some years is a good idea. Soybeans add soil nutrients that those other crops need to grow.

Toasted soybeans make a tasty snack. Soybeans can be turned into soymilk and used in granola bars. Soybeans can even be used to make ink.

# Follow the Farmer

The Great Plains gets busy at harvest time. Farmers like John start their day before sunrise. They have few breaks, working from sunup to sundown. Sometimes, they even work seven days a week. Let's take a look at John's workday during the wheat harvest.

**SUNRISE** After feeding the cows and pigs, I grab the day's eggs from the henhouse. I take a few of the eggs into the kitchen and eat a big breakfast. I usually look over my fields when the sun comes up to judge what needs to be done. Today, the wheat looks ready for harvesting.

**8:00 A.M.** I like to make sure I'm really comfortable when I climb into my combine. That's because I spend most of the day sitting in this machine. It got its name because it combines so many tasks, from cutting the wheat and separating it from the stalks to removing the husks that surround the grains.

**NOON** Sometimes things go wrong. Machine parts break, or, like today, the combine gets clogged up. When that happens, I have to fix the problem right then and there. Winter is coming, and the crops must be harvested. I don't have any time to lose. After making the repairs, I relax in the shade while I eat the two sandwiches I packed for lunch.

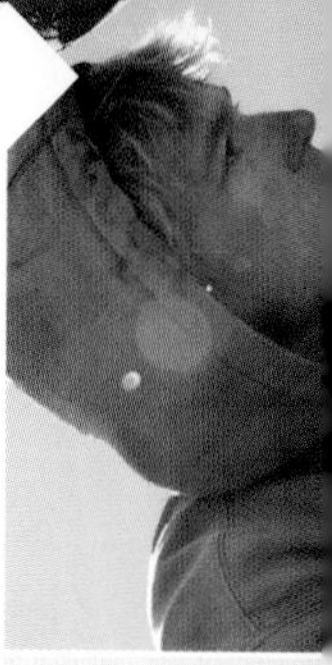

**4:00 P.M.** It's time for me to pump some of the grain into a waiting truck. I like to have the truck follow the combine into the field, so the combine never has far to go once it's full. When the grain is loaded, I will haul it to a storage facility where it will dry out and keep until I'm ready to sell on market day.

**9:00 P.M.** It's dark now, but I'm still at work. I want to finish up this section of my wheat fields. Combines have many lights on them because we farmers often work long into the night, especially during harvest. After this load of grain is moved to the truck, I'll eat a late dinner—then relax and spend time with my kids before getting to bed. Tomorrow's another busy day!

**Check In** What makes the Great Plains so good for farming?

**GENRE** Narrative

**Read to find out** about how farm families struggled to survive during the Dust Bowl.

# THE DUST BOWL

*by Becky Manfredini*

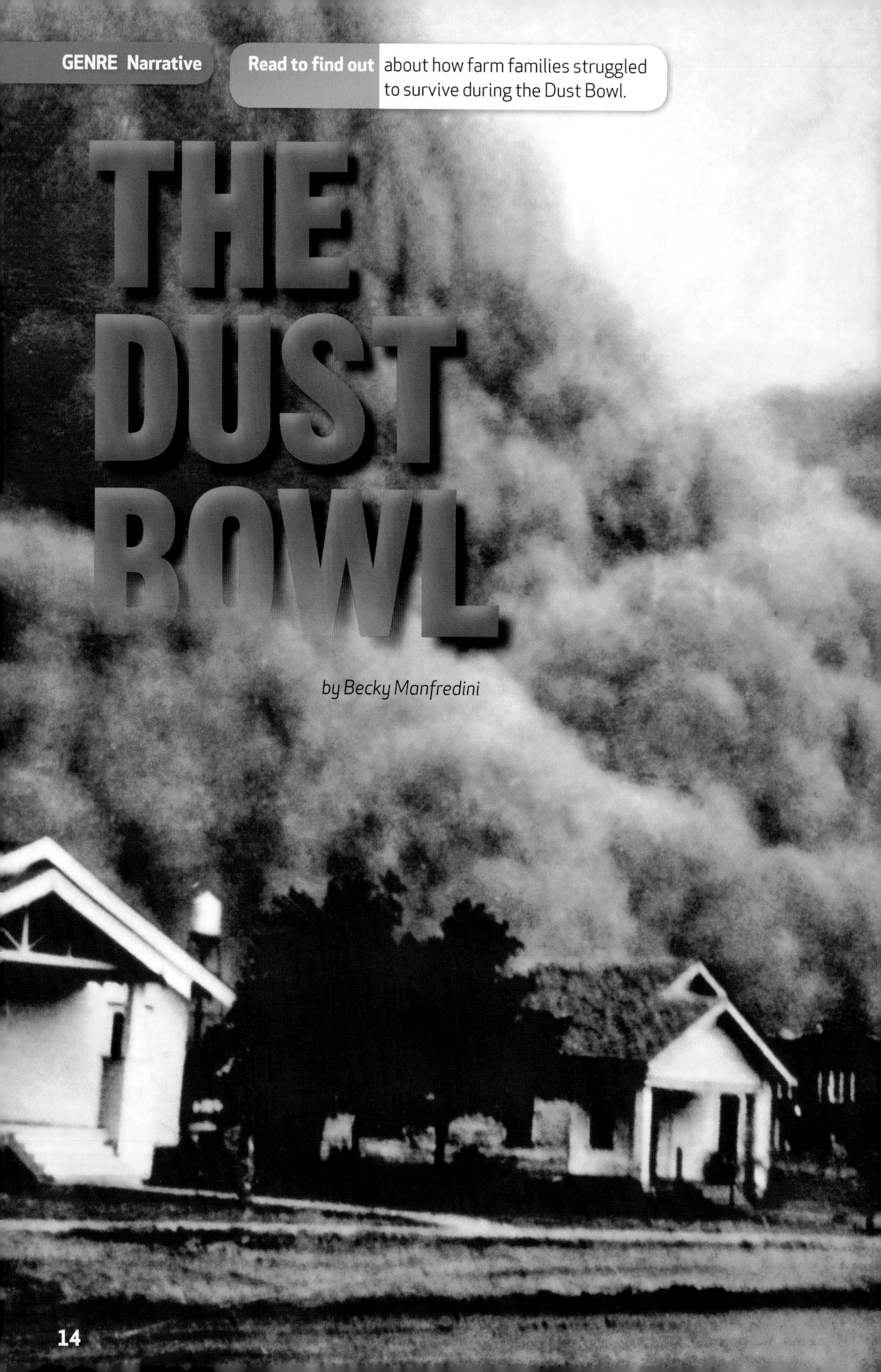

**"O BEAUTIFUL FOR SPACIOUS SKIES,
FOR AMBER WAVES OF GRAIN,
FOR PURPLE MOUNTAIN MAJESTIES,
ABOVE THE FRUITED PLAIN!"**

**—FROM "AMERICA THE BEAUTIFUL," BY KATHARINE LEE BATES**

In the early days of settling the Great Plains, this broad land truly was filled with "amber waves of grain." By the end of the 1920s, the farmers had planted millions of acres of wheat. In fact, they planted too much wheat. They overused the land, plowing and planting it too often. Constantly planting the same crop made the soil weak. But the worst was yet to come.

Just a few years later, a terrible **drought**, or period with little or no rain, hit the region. The crops dried up and died. Huge fields of wheat were destroyed. Even worse, the dried-out topsoil no longer had plants holding it in place. Winds picked up the loose, dry soil and blew it away in dust storms.

In 1935, newspaper reporters nicknamed the area suffering from the dust storms the **Dust Bowl**. This included parts of Colorado, Kansas, Texas, Oklahoma, and New Mexico. People soon used the term "Dust Bowl" to describe the time of the dust storms as well as the places hit by these storms.

Dark clouds of dirt blew hard and fast through small towns. They covered homes with a thick layer of dust.

# BLACK BLIZZARDS

Imagine you're outside in a blizzard with blowing snow stinging your face. You can't see anything but white. Now imagine the snow is black—and it's not cold outside. You're in a "black blizzard," the worst kind of dust storm. The people in the Dust Bowl could see a black blizzard coming. It was a huge, distant wall of black dirt that quickly rolled in. This cloud of dirt and dust swallowed up the sun's rays, bringing darkness.

The worst black blizzard happened on April 14, 1935. This report appeared in the *New Republic* magazine. It was written by Avis D. Carlson, who lived through the storm.

**The impact is like a shovelful of fine sand flung against the face. People caught in their own yards grope for the doorstep. Cars come to a standstill, for no light in the world can penetrate that swirling murk. . . . We live with the dust, eat it, sleep with it, watch it strip us of possessions and the hope of possessions.**

Richard Sell from Perryton, Texas, wrote this about the same day:

**Our mother . . . came running out of the house. She was frightened. She told us to get into the house immediately. . . . I looked to the northwest and saw a terrible, solid wall of rolling darkness approaching. Within minutes everything was dark, and the wind and dust were coming into the house everywhere. . . . That terrifying day is as clear in my mind as though it happened last year.**

The most powerful dust storms could carry millions of tons of soil across the Great Plains. The wind swept up the soil from farmland and scattered it far away.

A massive dust storm approached the town of Elkhart, Kansas, in 1937. The only safe place was behind closed doors once the storm reached the town.

It was dangerous to breathe the dust whipped up by a black blizzard. It was also very hard to escape it if you had to go outdoors.

# AFTER THE DUST SETTLED

After about eight years, the dust storms finally ended. But the suffering continued. Homes were ruined and crops failed. With no crops to sell, many families couldn't pay their banks what they owed for their land. The banks took back the land. In this way, many families lost their farms.

Thousands of desperate farm families headed west to California. As **migrant workers**, they traveled from farm to farm in search of steady work. Migrant workers moved often, going from place to place as crops were ready for harvesting.

Along country roads of the Great Plains in the 1930s, you could see people leaving their homes behind. They crammed what they could fit into their trucks or cars and drove away. Many people who lost their farms were too poor to own cars. So they hopped on moving trains headed to places where they might find work.

People everywhere were looking for jobs—but there weren't any. The government helped by starting programs like the Civilian Conservation Corps (CCC). The CCC workers planted rows of trees on the Great Plains to protect the soil from strong winds. Farmers were encouraged to leave some fields unplowed for a while. Leaving the land alone allowed the soil to rest and natural grasses to grow. These changes, over time, made the topsoil richer. The Dust Bowl period had taught farmers to take better care of the land.

In 1939, the rains finally came. The long drought ended. Once more, golden waves of wheat grew on the Great Plains.

This boy was careful to cover his nose and mouth during a dust storm.

Winds deposited loose soil in large drifts on this Kansas farm.

This farm family headed west. They hoped to find a better life there.

**Check In** What challenges did people face trying to survive on the Great Plains during the Dust Bowl?

**GENRE History Article** **Read to find out** about the brief history of the Pony Express.

# Neither Rain nor Sleet... NOR OUTLAWS

*by Jeff Osier*

This painting by Frank McCarthy shows a Pony Express rider. He is on his long ride between St. Joseph and Sacramento.

They galloped 2,000 miles across the Great Plains and high western mountains, from Missouri to California. They rode through territory claimed by Native Americans determined to defend their homelands. They faced thunderstorms and blizzards. They were tough, but light enough not to weigh a horse down. And they were not afraid of danger. These brave riders carried mail for the Pony Express. An **express** is any kind of system that delivers goods or messages quickly.

Many people were moving to California in the 1850s. The Pony Express provided mail service between this new state and the rest of the country. Until then, ships carried most mail to and from California. Ships had to sail around the southern tip of South America. That trip could take a month or longer.

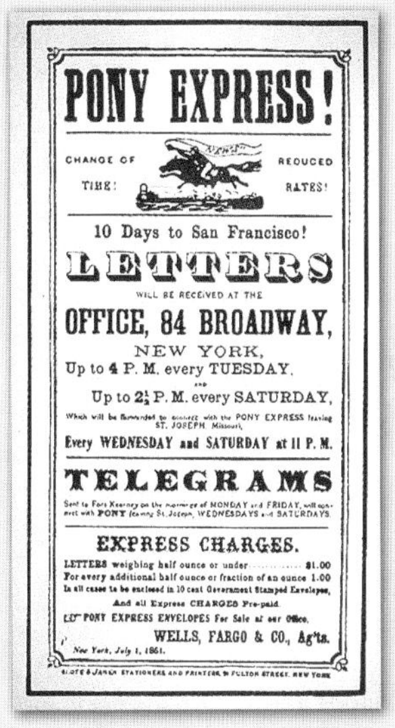


An advertisement for the Pony Express

The Pony Express came to the rescue. The route across land would be dangerous—but fast. It would deliver mail from St. Joseph, Missouri, to Sacramento, California, in only 10 days. This couldn't be done with one or a few riders. But it could be done using many riders and relay stations. A **relay** is the passing of something from one person to another. There were about 150 relay stations along the Pony Express route. A rider would ride from one station to the next. There, he would exchange his worn-out horse for a fresh one. After riding to a few stations, the rider would hand off the mail pouch to another rider, who would carry the mail a little farther.

# DELIVERING THE GOODS

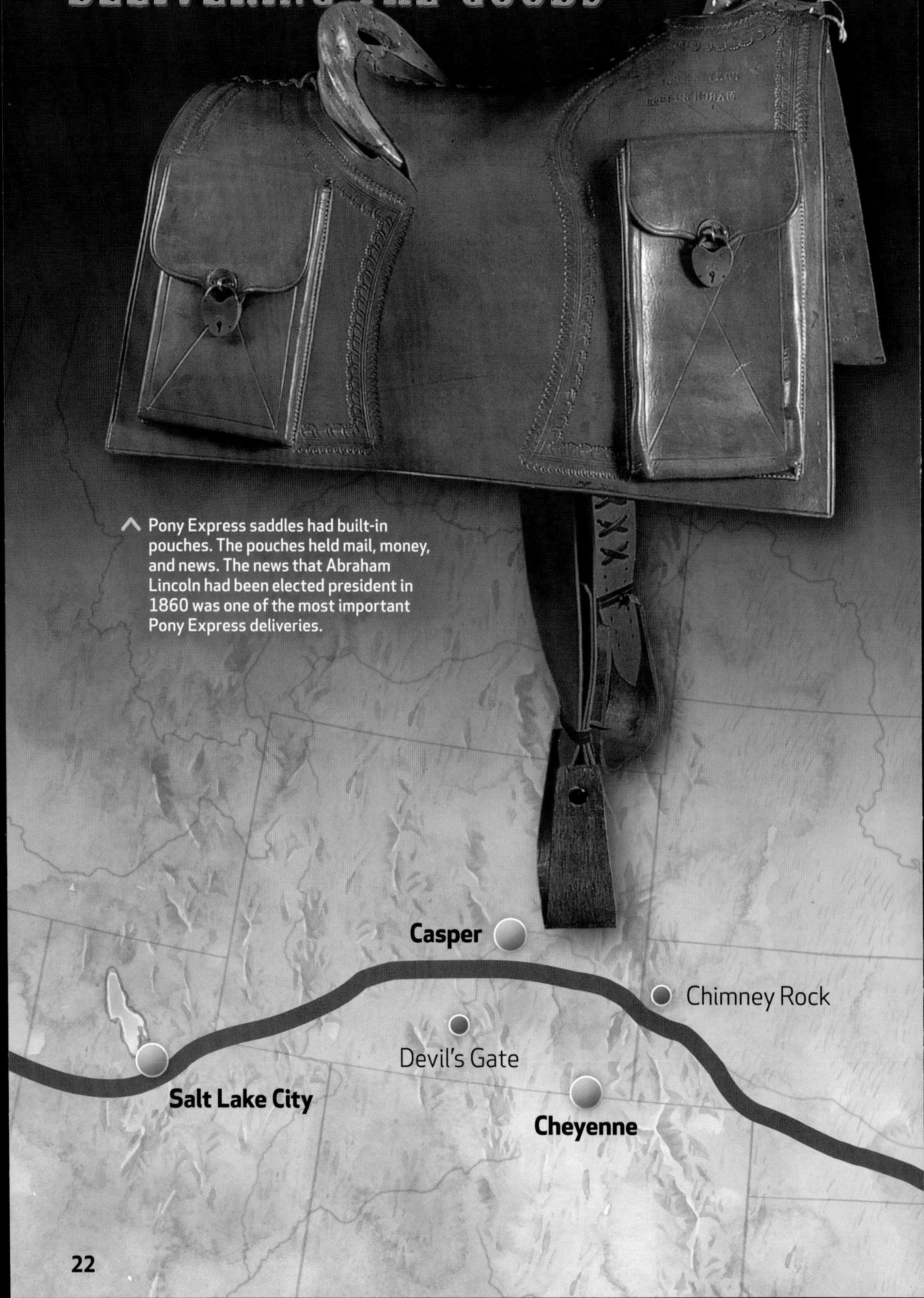


^ Pony Express saddles had built-in pouches. The pouches held mail, money, and news. The news that Abraham Lincoln had been elected president in 1860 was one of the most important Pony Express deliveries.

Pony Express riders faced dangers and **harsh**, or very rough, conditions every day. A rider like Johnny Fry (pictured below) might have described his day at work like this . . .

*The Pony Express oath says no swearing, no being unkind to the horses, and no fighting. But there was nothing in the oath saying I couldn't be scared!*

*Three days ago robbers attacked the Pony Express station at Rock Creek. They stole some of the horses and wounded poor Reynolds, who was tending the station while I was riding like mad toward Rock Creek!*

*I wasn't very far from the station when I heard the gunshot. I couldn't tell what direction it came from or even how close it was, so I just kept riding. When I got to Rock Creek, the robbers had just escaped, and the local doc was tending to Reynolds and his gunshot wound. I was shaken up, but I traded my worn-out horse for a fresh one and hit the trail again, keeping my eye out for trouble.*

*I made it to the next two stations before dark, and boy, was I glad to get to the end of my route in one piece. Now I'm beat and ready to sleep. But that gunshot I heard just before Rock Creek is still on my mind. Reynolds is lucky—he's going to be all right—but I sure hope I don't tangle with any robbers myself. No one's lost a mail pouch on this route yet, and I don't plan on being the first!*

No one is sure who rode the very first leg of the Pony Express route. Most people think it was Johnny Fry. On April 3, 1860, he set out from St. Joseph, Missouri. He was carrying the first pouch of mail to be delivered to Sacramento, California.

The Pony Express only lasted 18 months. Why did this service end? Blame it on the telegraph. This new invention sent messages over electrical wires. On October 24, 1861, telegraph wires finally connected the East Coast of the United States to the West Coast. With telegraph service, messages could be sent from New York to California in a matter of minutes. The Pony Express vanished, but it lives on in the legends of the Great Plains and the Wild West.

Fairbury

St. Joseph

Marysville

**Check In** What problem did the Pony Express solve?

GENRE Science Article

**Read to find out** how tornadoes form and are tracked.

# WILD WEATHER

by Becky Manfredini

## Welcome to Tornado Alley

Take cover. It's a twister! If you've watched the movie *The Wizard of Oz,* you probably remember Dorothy, her dog Toto, and their farmhouse. They were sucked up into a fierce whirlwind called a **tornado**. Although that story is make-believe, tornadoes can really cause terrible damage. A tornado can rip off roofs, uproot trees, and destroy anything in its path. Part of the Great Plains region is called Tornado Alley. That's because tornadoes tear through it fairly often without much warning.

What causes a tornado? During a severe thunderstorm, warm, moist air near the ground rises quickly into the colder clouds above. The warm air cools, and its moisture falls as strong rain and large hail. Meanwhile, air rushes in from all directions to fill the space the warm air left below. This air starts whirling around, and a funnel-shaped cloud forms. If the funnel cloud dips down all the way to the ground, it becomes a tornado. The inside of a tornado can suck up anything in its path. A tornado can last from only a few seconds to a few hours. But most twisters last about 10 minutes, which can seem like forever.

The area known as Tornado Alley is actually bigger than we thought. The "new" Tornado Alley has grown as our global climate has changed.

Many of the 1,000 tornadoes that strike in the United States each year happen in Tornado Alley in late spring or early fall. This tornado touched down on the plains of southeastern Colorado near the town of Campo.

Look at this whopper! Huge hailstones like this one can drop from the sky before a tornado.

## Tornado Tracking

We know how tornadoes form and where they strike most often. But how can we tell if one is headed our way? **Meteorologists** are scientists who study weather. Meteorologists warn us when bad weather is coming. They pay close attention to the temperature, wind speed, and moving air masses. They watch carefully for conditions that could lead to severe weather such as tornadoes. They are weather watchers and tornado trackers!

**Doppler radar** is a meteorologist's secret weapon. It sends out long, invisible radio waves that give meteorologists a picture of how dangerous a storm is and how fast it is moving. The radio waves hit clouds and **precipitation**, or water falling from the sky, Then the waves bounce back to the radar.

^ The Doppler radar tower at a National Weather Service Station

Doppler radar can also spot tornadoes. You've probably seen Doppler radar on TV or on a smartphone. Doppler maps are color-coded by how much rain is falling. They can show a storm moving across the screen, too.

Twisters can destroy whole towns in an instant. People need to be warned of an approaching tornado so they can seek cover. Every second counts. Meteorologists issue two kinds of messages about tornadoes. They send out a "tornado watch" when weather conditions could lead to a tornado. They send out a "tornado warning" when a tornado has been spotted. These weather messages help people stay tuned during watches and take cover during warnings. They save lives.

> A weather app on a smartphone can keep you alerted to dangerous weather.

# Meet a Storm Chaser

It's essential to take cover during tornadoes. However, National Geographic Explorer Tim Samaras didn't always do that. Tim bravely raced toward them! He was a storm chaser, and his job was to track down tornadoes to study them. He was also an electronics engineer. Tim designed new and improved weather probes—small instruments that he placed in a tornado's path. Some of the probes contained high-speed cameras that recorded video right inside the tornado. Probes help scientists like Tim understand how a tornado forms and determine how dangerous a particular tornado is.

Tim Samaras aims his van toward an approaching tornado.

## NATIONAL GEOGRAPHIC EXPLORER

**TIM SAMARAS** was the lead storm researcher for TWISTEX. That stands for the Tactical Weather Instrumented Sampling in or near Tornadoes Experiment. He used science, technology, engineering, and math skills to research tornadoes. Tim hoped that by better understanding tornadoes, he could help make more accurate tornado predictions. He wanted to help people prepare for when a tornado strikes.

As a tornado approached, Tim's probes would get sucked into the center of the whirlwind. Once there, they took many measurements in the lower part of the tornado.

From a safe distance, Tim examined the measurements from the probes. He used special programs on laptop computers set up in his van. The van was a weather station on wheels. A television antenna on the van's roof allowed him to watch satellite images and weather channel broadcasts. It also received global positioning system (GPS) information that told exactly where a storm was. Tim could even see lightning bolts and other amazing weather conditions through a special viewing window in the van's roof.

Tim Samaras often put himself in dangerous situations to make new discoveries about tornadoes. Sadly, Tim, his son Paul, and his research partner, Carl Young, were killed by a tornado on May 31, 2013. They were trying to collect scientific data about the powerful storm. Tim believed that if he could learn more, then maybe he could help improve our tornado warning systems.

# Severe Weather Pop Quiz

**Brilliant lightning flashes across a darkened sky. Thunderclaps boom. Hailstones smash the roofs of cars. In the distance, a twisting funnel cloud grows larger and darker. It roars like an approaching train. Suddenly it tears off the roof of a house and yanks a tree out of the ground. This is the power of a tornado in action.**

**Scientists know a lot about tornadoes and other severe weather. Still, there's a lot more to learn. There's also a lot of wrong information. Check out the following quiz to test your knowledge!**

## TRUE OR FALSE?

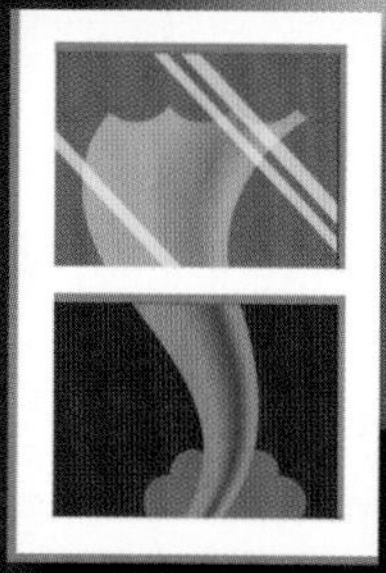

### *Open the windows to keep your house safe when a tornado is coming.*

**FALSE:** A tornado's high winds can damage a house whether the windows are closed or open.

### *A tornado can skip over houses, damaging one but not another.*

**TRUE:** A tornado may "bounce" up and down at random. You never know where it will land.

### *Lightning never strikes the same place twice.*

**FALSE:** Lightning is attracted to high, pointed structures. It often strikes them repeatedly.

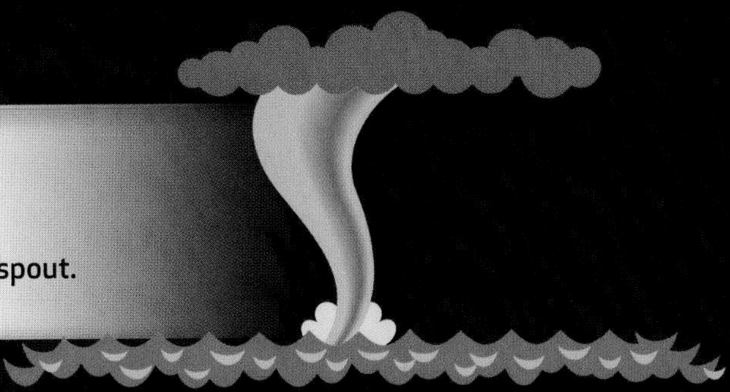

### *Tornadoes do not cross water.*

**FALSE:** A tornado over water is called a waterspout.

### *A basement, closet, or room in the center of a house is the safest place to be during a tornado.*

**TRUE:** And stay away from windows. Windows can break from the force of the wind. Glass will fly!

### *It's a good idea to seek shelter under an overpass or bridge during severe weather.*

**FALSE:** If a tornado forms, it can hit the bridge. You could be hit by flying debris. It's better to find a ditch or ravine and lie facedown in it.

### *A greenish-looking sky is always a sign of an approaching tornado.*

**FALSE:** A green sky means severe weather. That may or may not include a tornado.

### *A car can outrun a tornado.*

**FALSE:** A fast-moving car might be able to travel at about 80 miles per hour. But tornadoes can travel that quickly, too. They can also change directions suddenly. And they do not have to stay on the road or wait for traffic.

**Check In** How do meteorologists and storm chasers use technology to learn about tornadoes?

## Discuss

1. What connections can you make among the five selections in this book? How are the selections related?

2. What are some of the challenges and opportunities that are part of living on the Great Plains?

3. How does reading the real-life accounts of people who lived through the black blizzards help you understand what happened during the Dust Bowl?

4. How have the ways that people communicate changed since the time of the Pony Express?

5. What do you still wonder about the Great Plains and the topics discussed in the book?